A Teacher's Insight

Teaching inspired poetry

For my family and friends - thank you for your words of encouragement and support along the way!

A special thanks to Emma Robinson, author of https://www.facebook.com/motherhoodforslackers who inspired me to start writing again.

CONTENTS

Dear Parent

I understand that you are scared
To wave your child goodbye
And leave him in a teacher's hands
Don't worry if you cry!

I'm used to weeping parents
It's hard to leave I know.
But it's time to share him (just a bit)
To help him learn and grow.

Let me reassure you
That I'll give your child my best
I'll wipe his tears, soothe his fears
And change his dirty vest!

If your darling child is full of cold
I'll blow his nose all day
Just like you, I'll care for him
In a special way.

I'll treat him like I would my own
I'll catch him from a fall
And if there's ANY problem
I'll be sure to tell you all.

It's true he'll grow to love us
He'll talk of school a lot
It doesn't mean he hates you
And that you should lose the plot!

I'll tell you a secret…
That when your boy is here
He talks to me as much of you
Of this please have no fear.

You'll always be his mother
Whilst teachers come and go
To him you are his number one
This I truly know.

Soon you'll see some changes
In your little girl or boy
They'll become more independent
And to see this, it's a joy!

I'll teach them all I have to give
To share, climb and to write
But to you they safely will return
To tuck them in at night.

With love from a teacher…

Children vs Teacher

On Monday, I cried for an hour or two
Then screamed at the teacher and threw my shoe

On Tuesday, I pretended to be a goat
Then had a tantrum about wearing my coat

On Wednesday, I coloured in all of my face
Then made a dash for it out of the place

On Thursday, I bumped my head on the floor
Then did a big wee as I stood by the door

On Friday, I emptied a tub of glitter
Then went to play with some dirty litter

On Monday, one kid just wouldn't stop crying
My head started thumping, I thought I was dying!

On Tuesday, the class sounded just like a farm
Then one naughty child took a bite from my arm

On Wednesday, I had some cleaning to do
Then I followed a child who needed a poo

On Thursday, I spent the day using ice
Then mopping the floor - not once, but twice

On Friday, I thought this has got to be it
As one little child got as dirty as...

The Nativity

Joseph's lost his tea towel
Mary looks a sight
The donkey can't stop yawning
He was up for half the night.
A wise man has his finger
Right inside his nose
One angel's got an angry face
She doesn't like her clothes!
King Herod is now crying
Because he needs a wee
The shepherd's hitting all his sheep
And Gabriel starts to flee
The camel has a breakdown
And won't go on the stage
We cheer and clap them anyway
They're just that funny age!

Why I don't miss marking

My desk is full of highlighters, teacher's stamps and more
My daily job has just begun when it reaches half past four
With thirty children in my class and four long lessons daily
That's 120 books to mark - I think I might go crazy!

Now every school has a different code, in mine we mark with stamps
Green means 'great', orange means 'ok' and red means 'God help this child he doesn't stand a chance'
Ofsted wants each bit of work to have a useful phrase
But seriously, my kids can't read or understand their grades

I waste my time each evening, doing what I know I should
All the work has comments, more than saying 'Good'
In theory, every child should see exactly what I write
But, if I sat down showing them, I'd be there throughout the night!

My breaks are spent with marking pens
At lunch, I use the stickers
I barely have much time to breathe
I might just wet my knickers

Just when I think I've got it sussed
S for spelling mistake, H for handwriting and the like
The head calls a new meeting and much to our surprise
The marking system has been changed - you should hear the cries!

Please don't eat the playdough

Please don't eat the playdough
Or wipe your nose on there
Please don't pee upon the mat
Then act like you don't care

Please don't chew the crayons
Or cut the new girl's hair
Please don't scream and run inside
Or swing upon your chair

Please don't try to hold my hand
I've seen where that hand's been
You've sat with that one down your pants
I doubt it's really clean

Please don't bang your head again
I'll have to phone your mum
Then she'll give me evils
And stop you having fun

Please don't bring that toy to school
You know you cannot share
Don't come in wearing laces
I like your velcro pair!

Please don't take your hair out
Roughly every hour
Or bite your friend upon his arm
Because he broke your tower

Please don't take the teacher's stamp
To decorate your mate
Or try to plan the great escape
Over the school gate

Please don't do a roly-poly
Outside, on the ground
Don't pick up worms and insects,
Then show me what you've found

Please don't waddle out the loo
With your pants around your feet
Or give your dirty tissue
As if it was a treat

Please don't scoff your biscuit down
So quickly that you choke
Or make me say your name ten times
My voice will start to croak

You make it hard to like you
It's a good job that you're cute
When you sit upon my knee
And your bum goes toot toot toot!

Now if somehow you do these things
I guess I'll understand
After all, you're only three
And teaching kids is grand.

Just his teacher

You think I'm just his teacher
But in fact I'm so much more
There is a lot that you don't see
Behind this classroom door.

He runs to me each morning
And greets me with a smile
I'm warmed to see his happiness
As if he were my child.

I hurt when he is hurting
And jump ecstatically
When at last your boy has learnt
How to count to three.

I try to teach him right from wrong
And do the best I can
So that he can grow to be
A truly special man.

I'll think of him when he is gone
And miss his funny ways
The moments I have shared with him
I'll remember all my days.

Thank you for my time with him
It really was a pleasure
He's made me laugh when I was down
Your son's a little treasure!

Friday

There's a hole in my new trousers
That was made there by a child.
We've been playing 'hairdressers'
So I'm looking pretty wild.
I've caught a cold from one kid
And a lovely runny eye.
There are chalk prints on my bottom
But please don't ask me why.
There is paint right up my left arm,
Some stickers in my hair
And green glitter in my eyebrows
But, it's Friday - I don't care!

December

Christmas time is nearing
Teachers are all wrecked
The kids are turning wild
The school hall is truly 'decked'
Cleaners start to anger
As glitter season's here
The Nativity is looming
And the tension's really clear
Though there's work still to be done
The kids just cannot cope
They're dreaming now of Christmas
And of snow upon the slope

Miss

Miss, I want my mummy!
Miss, I need a poo
Miss, here's a broken crayon
Please Miss, tie my shoe
Miss, I've hurt my finger
Miss, We've just bumped heads
Miss, did you hear the naughty word
That the new boy said?
Miss, I need a tissue
Miss, I've lost my hat
Miss, she swallowed playdough
And that boy just called me fat
Miss, I've dropped my hair clip
And it's fallen down the loo
I've only done a pee pee
I can't reach it - can you?
Miss, my tummy's aching
Miss, I've found this drawing pin
Miss, she took my picture
And she put it in the bin
Miss, is this the answer?
Miss, have I spelled this right?
Miss, an owl's nocturnal
And it stays up through the night!
Miss, my Mum has lost my book
Miss, can you peel my fruit?
Miss, he kicked me just like this
With his welly boot
Miss, is it now lunch time?
Miss, do I have to wear my coat?

I've tipped the sand tray into water
To see if it will float
Miss, I've got the hiccups
Miss, he did a fart
Miss, he took my aeroplane
And he's pulled it all apart.
Kids I have a headache
Sort things out yourself
I'll be in the stock room
Staring at the shelf!

Let the term begin

We are not ready
For the term to begin
Please just one more week
Don't let the kids in!

But it starts again
As they bolt through the door
Acting like loonies,
Worse than before!

My class may forget
That they like me at all
They'll cling to their mums
As if they were small

The crying will start
And I'll wish I was still
Back on my sofa
Avoiding this 'thrill'

The kids will relax
As they're lured by the toys
They'll speak of Santa
And start to make noise.

Of course half the kids
Will return with the flu
Or a tummy bug
Bringing sick and poo!

Then one child will smile
And all will be well
For I love my job
I've missed them - don't tell!

School Trip

We've packed ten tonne of wet wipes
And a sick bag for the bus
But no teacher sleeps the night before
They're dreading all the fuss!

There was bound to be one parent
Who rolled up really late
It's nine o'clock already
We were meant to leave at eight!

All the kids are counted
But they total twenty nine
Some forget to bring their lunch
I hope that I've got mine!

At last the bus gets going
And the kids are acting wild
I confiscate a load of sweets
From each and every child.

We get there and it's raining
We're grateful it's inside
Until I saw revolving doors
And then I nearly cried!

The place ain't made for children
All the kids now need the loo
We find a single cubicle
The kids - there's thirty -two!

A lady started talking
But my kids just didn't care
They started running riot
And were darting everywhere!

The tour itself did not go well
One child bumped his head
Then he acted falling down
I thought that he was dead!

The class were told they could not touch
Of course, they touched the lot
Seven kids lost their playtime
Me - I lost the plot!

We headed back onto the bus
The kids began to sing
By the time that I got home
I couldn't hear a thing!

Trips from school are so much fun
I want to tell the Head
Next time I will stay at home
Faking sick instead!

Ofsted

The phone call came, the staff were silent,
The head looked like he might turn violent!
Actions stations, go go go!
We were quizzed on things we ought to know.
To our classrooms we all went.
To sort, display or simply vent,
'Why us? We've been through this before!'
We had some coffee, cried and swore!
All planning had to be in order.
My cupboards showed that I'm a hoarder.
That night we left at half past ten.
At six, we all were in again!
Hoping, praying that we weren't first,
Or last - perhaps this would be worse!
We begged the children to be good,
Bribing them the best we could.
Then my time came and I tried to smile,
Whilst thinking, 'Please God- don't quiz THAT child'
I gave some kids the look of death
And whispered 'stop' under my breath.
At last my class was left alone.
Later, it was time for the head to moan.
Of course the teachers all survived,
But I'm off to work at the McDrive!

That boy

When home time comes I hand him over - he doesn't want to go
A tear rolls down my cheek because of all the things I know

At night I cannot sleep at all for thinking of that boy
I bet at home he doesn't own a single book or toy

He comes to school not having ate and never looks his best
I find him breakfast from the kitchen and let him have a rest

He doesn't want to learn at school, he wants only to be seen
So I try to give him my attention and teach the others in-
between

I won't ask him for his reading book, I know full well it's lost
He needs a bigger jumper but he can't afford the cost

Those marks he didn't do himself, the dirt it never goes
No child should ever have to live, having that boy's woes

I want to take him home with me to keep him safe from harm
But all I can do is make some calls to try to raise alarm

Celebs at School

Each day at school I have a treat
With new celebs I get to meet
There's Batman who just picks his nose
And likes to wet through all his clothes.
There's Cinderella who stamps her feet,
She scowls at all the kids she meets.
There's Spiderman who is never still.
He jumps off chairs just for the thrill.
Then there's the Incredible Hulk
Who spends his days in a terrible sulk.
The Frozen Princess can't use a chair.
She has no concept of how to share.
Iron man likes to use his weight,
To push and poke at those he hates.
Donald Duck makes noise ALL day
The teachers cheer when he's away.
At school I am the sanest one
They call me teacher Atilla the Hun!

What The Parents Say

Just thought I'd ring to let you know my daughter's lost her pretty bow. Last time she ate one, didn't I say? In hospital she had to stay.

We've started potty training, but he hasn't got a clue so I've brought him here to make your day and leave this up to you.

My daughter's got a real bad cold, in fact she cannot breathe, but she wanted to come in today, I'm sure you'll be relieved.

Here's his sun cream, rub it in at least ten times a day and make him go the toilet lots, as when he needs it, he doesn't say!

Yes he was sick two times last night but I thought that it had passed. I didn't tell you when I dropped him off- I thought I'd send a fax.

My girl is really quiet at home, she never makes a fuss. She wouldn't spend the entire day making noises like a bus!

That goo you see there near his eye is really not contagious. No, he hasn't seen a doctor - stop being so outrageous!

What's that tiny mark I see? Just there on his knee... in his pocket I've only given him a rock, two guns and a key.

I forgot to bring her change of clothes but I'm sure you've got some spare. Of course, I'll never bring them back because I just don't care.

My boy is not himself today, he hasn't slept at all. I've brought him here anyway - I know he'll have a ball.

He needs a harder reading book, he's really rather clever. You clearly haven't studied much and I won't trust you - ever!

Parent's evening - can I bring my child? Can you do next
Wednesday too? I haven't been for the last five years
Because I had the flu!

I'd like to see them try!

At half past nine I go to bed
And people ask me why.
They think my job is easy
But, I'd like to see them try!

"Miss, Miss", I hear 100 times,
Before I'm through the door.
The kids make lots of small demands
I simply can't ignore.

I have to be their Mum, their Dad,
The good cop and the bad.
The noise a class of kids can make
Would make the sanest mad.

My pocket's full of tissues
To catch a snotty nose
Before that child runs past my chair
And wipes it on my clothes!

I pull my hair out teaching them
That 1 add 1 is 2.
They stare at me with black expressions,
They just don't have a clue!

So I try a different way
To get the kids on-board

I buy the whole of Asda
Getting stuff I can't afford.

Getting children into coats,
Their scarves, gloves and their hats.
Is like wrestling with an octopus
Or perhaps some angry cats.

I sing and dance and play the fool
And jump about all day.
I act the entertainer,
So the kids don't run away.

If I find a spider
I have to reassure
That these things are lovely
As I chuck it out the door!

The kids cry in the morning
As they wan't to stay with Mum
But when it comes to home time
They won't leave, they're having fun!

On the mat

Kindly sit down on the mat,
Now's not the time to have a chat.
Don't poke him in the back like that
Or make weird noises like a cat.

Try your best not to wriggle,
Break some wind, then start to giggle.
I don't want to have to niggle,
But why must you ALWAYS fiddle?

Put your hand up, please don't shout.
Listen to what we talk about.
Don't give your friend a friendly clout,
Then look as if your guilt's in doubt!

When your hands are wet with peach
Don't play with all the things in reach,
Or lick that boy like you're a leech
It's like a zoo I'm trying to teach!

The Teaching Assistant

I wasn't the best helper
That the school had ever had
From what I can remember
I was really rather bad

To start off every morning
I'd be told about the day
Then be sent off to make copies
To the office down the way

Most mornings I'd take half an hour
To get the copies done
The machine would break ten seconds in
And I'd beg for help to come

If the teacher asked for ten on pink
I'd return with eight on blue
Unless I wrote it down you see
I wouldn't have a clue!

One day I filed the children's work
I truly did my best
Of course I'd done it wrongly
And left the teacher with a mess

After working there just for a year
I realised that I sucked
So I trained to be a teacher
And now I'm really_____!

I tried to be…

I tried to be the teacher
That the kids would surely miss
But I found myself just shouting
And sometimes I'd even hiss

I tried to be so patient
With a smile upon my face
But when the kids annoyed me
I would go somewhere and pace

I tried to be a person
Who was always firm but fair
But it was harder that I thought
To teach young kiddies how to share

I tried to make the children laugh
And have some fun at school
But it was tough to get the balance right
Whist sticking to the rules

I tried to be the best teacher
I knew that I could be
But I've learnt I'm only human
And it's best to just be me!

Staff Meetings

The meetings come but once a week
But every one is scary
We dread to hear what's coming next
We just survive them - barely!

Every week there's some bad news
Some more tasks to be done
Most of them aren't useful
And none of them are fun!

Sometimes I wonder what's for tea
Whilst I just nod and smile
Hoping if a question's asked
It isn't for a while

I look around at other staff
And think 'Is it just me?'
Or are these meetings causing stress
And endless misery?

One meeting was so horrid
That I wanted to just die
I wondered if I could go home
If I began to cry!

So I left the school with a list in hand
Of things I had to do
But which highlighter was I meant to use?
The pink one or the blue?

We're often told of new assessments
And boxes to be filled
Whoever thought of these ideas
Really should be killed!

I want you to remember…

I want you to remember that you're going to be a star,

Remember every morning just how wonderful you are,

Remember you can do it, even when you think it's hard,

Remember you can make a friend, if you let down your guard,

Remember not to cry each time that things don't go your way,

Remember to be happy and to take some time to play,

Remember that you're gorgeous, even when you're told you're not

Remember that you will be missed and I loved you a lot!

About the Author

Leonie Roberts is an English graduate and pre-school teacher who is currently living and working in Italy. She works with wonderful staff and children who give her daily inspiration for her writing.

Last year, Leonie set up a Facebook page entitled, 'A Teacher's Insight', where she posts funny stories and poetry about the joys of teaching young children.

Leonie is also busy working on some children's picture book stories, which she hopes to publish in the coming years...watch this space! Coming from Liverpool, Leonie would love nothing more than to return to her home town to promote her work.

To follow Leonie's Facebook page, please visit https://www.facebook.com/ateachersinsight.
Her other work can be found on Authonomy.com, including the stories 'The Witch Who Wanted To Walk' and 'Bianca and the Blue Scooter'.
Please note that it is completely free to join this site to review her work and any support would be greatly appreciated.

25760442R00020

Printed in Great Britain
by Amazon